The Laws of Entrepreneurship

"Unlocking Your Way To Success"

Michael McCain

The Laws Of Entrepreneurship

Michael McCain

The Laws Of Entrepreneurship

Michael McCain

Although the author and publisher have made every effort to ensure that the information in this book was correct at press time, the author and publisher (Maximize Publishing Inc. & Dr. Michael McCain) do not assume and hereby disclaim any liability to any party for any loss, damage, or disruption caused by errors or omissions, whether such errors or omissions result from negligence, accident, or any other cause.

The names and identifying characteristics of certain individuals referenced in this publication have been changed. This publication contains the opinions and ideas of its author. It is sold with the understanding that neither the author nor the publisher is engaged in rendering legal, tax, investment, insurance, financial, accounting, or other professional advice or services. If the reader requires such advice or services, a competent professional should be consulted. Relevant laws vary from state to state. The strategies outlined in this book may not be suitable for every individual, and are not guaranteed or warranted to produce any particular results.

No warranty is made with respect to the accuracy or completeness of the information contained herein, and both the author and publisher specifically disclaim any responsibility for any liability, loss, or risk, personal or otherwise, which is incurred as a consequence, directly

The Laws Of Entrepreneurship
Michael McCain

or indirectly, of the use and application of any of the contents of this book.

Maximize Publishing Inc.

2018 Monterey Ave

Bronx N.Y. 10457

Attn.: Michael McCain

C/O: Kevin Brown

© 2013 by Maximize Publishing Inc. & Dr. Michael McCain Enterprises Inc.

All rights reserved, including the right to reproduce this book

Or portions thereof in any form whatsoever. Any Reproduction of this book in recording, print or otherwise is punishable by law and copy right standards. For any information or contact with the author you may write the above named address.

ISBN-13:
978-1484928806

ISBN-10:
1484928806

The Laws Of Entrepreneurship

Michael McCain

Table of Contents:

Dedication..................................9

Introduction...............................11

Laws of Entrepreneurship............13

Other Books By The Author...........53

About The Author........................55

The Laws Of Entrepreneurship
Michael McCain

The Laws of Entrepreneurship

"Unlocking Your Way To Success"

Michael McCain

The Laws Of Entrepreneurship

Michael McCain

Dedication

I would first like to thank my students at "Entrepreneurs University". I would also like to thank my partners at Maximize Publishing Inc. I would like to thank every entrepreneur that has been inspired by my work to achieve greater in their lives and reach for their goals and success. I would also like to thank my family who has stood by my side and believed in my dream when no one else did. I would like to thank my mentors such as Dr. E. Bernard Jordan, Dr. Walter E. Holmes, and Dr. Gary L. Chance who all played a very vital and important role into the person that I have both become and developed into.

Special thanks to Mary Moorer, George Moorer, Kelby Lott, Kevin Brown, Michelle Cruz, April Rivera, and Dr. Michelle Davis. Because of your prayers and strong support I have made it this far. Thank you!

Introduction

I encourage every entrepreneur who holds this book in their hands to take the keys and principles written in this book seriously. This book has been designed to empower continuing entrepreneurs as well as neonate entrepreneurs who are just getting their feet wet with starting a business or building a brand. The keys in this book will empower you to align your day to day task, skills, know-how, wit and ability to perform as an entrepreneur should. I called it the laws of entrepreneurship because it is a foundation that anyone can build from, it opens key principles that every entrepreneur should learn and know for themselves entering into the business world.

Each key and principle will show you a stepping stone to build on. It will also expose any flaws or areas where you may need further improvement as you set out to become a successful entrepreneur. This book is not designed to provide 25 keys/ principles I call "the laws of entrepreneurship" others may call them quick tips, no matter your preference it is designed for quick and witty insight for business matters. If you so desire more in-depth teaching please take time to invest in "The Newborn Entrepreneur," from which these laws were formed into this mini book. Also check out "The Millionaire Class" both are aids designed for entrepreneurial empowerment.

The Laws of Entrepreneurship

In my recent years I spent allot of time meditating on what success meant to me. Year after year I believe that my definition evolved, it didn't out right change. It was experiences and new knowledge that added to the depth of my definition. As a matter of fact, one of the highest contributors was my experiences with failure. It is common that when we battle with things we fail at we will start looking at our lives differently. During this mental battle with my failures and achievements in life I summed up what I felt the total of success meant to me, "success is the sum total of the consistency of purpose".

As a neonate entrepreneur you have to stay in line with things that mean something to you. Your diligence and consistency is the key to what defines and builds lasting success in your life. Not only will it build the success you are looking for but it will mold your character, skills and habits which are the other contributors to your success. Regardless of your definition of success, there are, oddly enough, a great number of common characteristics that are shared by successful business people. We will outline those characteristics in depth in this chapter so hang tight.

The Laws of Entrepreneurship are a set of laws that are promised to work for the person who is looking to become a fortune 500 company, to the person who is looking to start a local business or successful stay at home business. While this chapter is rich with tips and principles that you will want to live by and remember it is a chapter that really sounds like a book of its own.

1. ***Do what you enjoy, Do what you love*** One of the keys to a successful business is to do something you love doing. I've attended countless entrepreneurship summits and conferences to hear this truth over and over again. At first I ignored it, but as time went on is started watching people go into business doing things for the sake of money and failing. I also saw people who began to be unhappy with their

work. Entrepreneurship in my opinion has always been about doing what you love, you gain personal satisfaction from growing a business out of what you love. When you're doing what you love, no matter how fast or slow the business is growing you never lose the passion because it's something that you love. When you're in business only for the money you quickly start to lose interest and your focus fades and you begin looking for the next quick opportunity. When you don't enjoy what you're doing it is likely that it will begin to show in the success or failure of your business. The failure that some entrepreneur's face is the loss of passion while building their business. Sometimes that loss of passion comes by not counting up the cost, and not having resources and mentoring.

2. Take what you do seriously –

Pursuing the road to becoming a successful entrepreneur you have to pull your expectations into alignment and focus on believing in your dream. In other words simply put, **you have to believe in yourself!** (That includes believing in whatever service product or goods you sell. Trust that you're performing at top quality and providing a quality product). You have to keep your foot to the grind stone and not become lax in your business dealings. Too many people that pursue home based entrepreneurship become lax and fall behind in sales or performance. When you begin to lax in performance you leave yourself open as a target. When people come along that don't believe in what you're doing you will be easily moved or discouraged because your performance is out of alignment.

There are people who don't believe you're a business owner if you don't have an office or perform your work out of such as an office building, store front and etc. Little do people know home based entrepreneurs make good money and it is an industry that has grown by leaps and bounds in recent years.

3. Plan Everything

No matter if you have a home based business, store front, factory or office building, you have to take what you do seriously and make it a matter of such importance that it requires a plan. You need to develop a plan that you can implement and maintain. Business planning is no joke, it's so important because it requires you to analyze each business situation, do you're research and put together all your data.

Business planning is practically your second step. It's a well thought out plan as to how your business will operate and work. I learned the importance of this as I began to grow as an entrepreneur because I found myself having a big and vast vision needing to learn how to trust people to help me fulfill the vision of my business. I also had to learn how to identify people who would be suitable to work with my vision or serve it. Having a business plan allowed me to be able to employ the right people as well as give them a guide to follow as to how our system works.

Business planning allows you to measure the success and failures of your business. How well you're doing and where you may be failing at. Sometimes your plans can be edited or change, improved to what works for you or what works for the business more importantly.

4. *Manage Your Money-*

The pulse that sets the tone for the thriving business is cash flow. You need money to run and operate your business no matter how large or small your business is. You need to buy inventory, pay for services, promote and market your business, repair or replace equipment and pay yourself (or employees) so that you can continue your work.

So everyone from the small business owner to the million dollar entrepreneur needs to become wise in their affairs with handling money. You need to be financially wise with money to ensure that cash keeps flowing in. To be sure that your business is growing in profits and not just surviving. When you first start a business it will take a while before you see a significant profit. Yet you have to maintain your work and your finances and stay away from any gray areas or the invisible red line.

Money Management outlines:

A.   The money you receive from clients in exchange for your goods and services you provide.
      (Income)

B.   The Money you spend on inventory, supplies, wages and other items required to keep your business operating.
      (Expenses)

C.   The Books: keeping honest and correct books to show expenses and payouts for management purposes and tax payer information.

5. *The Art of Sales* –

Any entrepreneur in business needs to grow the skill of making a sale; from the product, to the service and building returning clientele. The fact that I have found is when you do what you do well the word will spread and word of mouth brings you better business than paying top dollars for advertising. As a matter of fact, advertising usually just makes your company's image look big but leads to very little sales. If you really want to make a sale you have to do it the old fashion way and be knowledgeable, personable and genuine and **just ask for the sale**! That does not mean that advertising, marketing, branding and other useful tools are a complete waste. It just leads to very few sales. Just remember to be genuine and forward (not demanding) and ask for the sale.

6. Know Your Customers

When you're in business you have to know your demographic which is your client base and market; you also have to remember to make your clients a matter of importance. Sometimes entrepreneurs can be guilty of venturing off into finding their own pleasures and forgetting about the customers. Don't become engulfed with making the product/brand so excellent that you forget to add value and quality to your service, also look out for updates and changes to accommodate your changing market and demographic.

Your business is all about your customers, or clients, period. After all, your customers are the people that will ultimately decide if your business goes boom or bust. You can leave an imprint of care and excellence with each interaction with your customers/clients that will guarantee a reference or return. It's the make or breaker law with customers/clientele. Everything you do in business must be customer focused, including your policies, warranties, payment options, operating hours, presentations, advertising and promotional campaigns and website. In addition, you must know who your customers are inside out and upside down.

7. Marketing & Branding

Every entrepreneur needs to brand his or herself. You need to define your brand by the quality and the service you bring. You also need to have a unique image about your product or service that makes you stand out amid all the other companies who may be doing the self-same thing as you do. If you brand and market yourself correctly you will create a lasting impression as well as a memorable one. Out of all the companies your client can choose from they will always remember you.

You have to learn the art of self-promotion and not rely on hiring too many companies to do the talking and marketing for you. Also learn to market yourself without being obnoxious and annoying because customers will become easily turned off and look elsewhere to perform their business and duties. Along with your marketing you need to build a positive image about your business. Allow some of the truth and best qualities about your business to be highlighted in your marketing and branding. Remember to always project an image of excellence and professionalism.

8. Advance With Technology-

We live in a world that is changing all the time. Technology is improving all the time and the mom and pop way of doing business is slowly becoming a thing of the past. Entrepreneurs must balance how they approach adding technology to their business by adding changes when necessary but not going overboard. It's OK to explore new options as they become available but as long as they fit your brand and your image. Never use something that will make you look like a misfit.

9. Every Business Needs A Team

There are no super heroes when it comes to entrepreneurship. One of the tell-tell signs of a business headed for failure is a business without a team, support or partnerships. Even if you are operation a s-corp. (sole proprietorship) where you are the only owner, you will still need to contract workers to provide services and partner with people to make accomplishments that you're unable to do. Or even hire people to work under you while you attend to other areas of the business. The point is, you need a team!

No one person can build a successful business completely alone. You will need people that are as committed as you are to making sure the business succeeds in its endeavors. People who are as passionate about your work as you are and take the company seriously. Your business team may include family members, friends, suppliers, business alliances, employees, sub-contractors, industry and business associations, local government and the community.

Last but definitely not the least is your customers and clients are among the most important people apart of your team. Your customers are the deciding factor on the changes, progression, success, failure and future of the business, they encompass that much power!

10. Become known as an expert.

When you have a problem that needs to be solved, do you seek just anyone's advice or do you seek an expert in the field to help solve your particular problem? Obviously, you want the most accurate information and assistance that you can get. You naturally seek an expert to help solve your problem. You call a plumber when your pipes leak, a real estate agent when it's time to sell your home or a dentist when you have a toothache. Therefore, it only stands to reason that the more you become known for your expertise in your business, the more people will seek you out to tap into your expertise, creating more selling and referral opportunities.

When I first began working on writing out tips, ideas, strategies and concepts to help other authors improve their work I had already begun to receive calls requesting my insight and input on peoples projects. People began to watch my work and my work was speaking for me. People took note that I kept publishing books and with each book came some significant strides in my success. You can achieve the same by working on your expertise and forming it into a business or product/service that can be sold. In effect, becoming known as an expert is another style of prospecting for new business, just in reverse. Instead of finding new and qualified people to sell to, these people seek you out for your expertise.

11. Create a competitive advantage.

A home business must have a clearly defined unique selling proposition. This is nothing more than a fancy way of asking the vital question, "Why will people choose to do business with you or purchase your product or service instead of doing business with a competitor and buying his product or service?" In other words, what one aspect or combination of aspects is going to separate your business from your competition? Will it be better service, a longer warranty, better selection, longer business hours, more flexible payment options, lowest price, personalized service, better customer service, better return and exchange policies or a combination of several of these? These were some of the determining factors I had to place together along with my business plan for reaching my success.

12. Invest in yourself.

You have to learn how to invest in your mind. Purchasing educational material that will help you build your expertise as well as your skills and abilities. Top entrepreneurs buy and read business and marketing books, magazines, reports, journals, newsletters, websites and industry publications, knowing that these resources will improve their understanding of business and marketing functions and skills. At first I must admit that it took me a while to get into the swing of investing into reading materials and magazines.

Join business associations and clubs, and network with other skilled business people to learn their secrets of success and help define their own goals and objectives. Top entrepreneurs attend business and marketing seminars, workshops and training courses, even if they have already mastered the subject matter of the event. They do this because they know that education is an ongoing process. There are usually ways to do things better, in less time, with less effort. In short, top entrepreneurs never stop investing in the most powerful, effective and best business and marketing tool at their immediate disposal-- themselves. Staying connected to key organizations and institutions is key.

13. *Be accessible.*

We're living in a time when we all expect our fast food lunch at the drive-thru window to be ready in mere minutes, our money to be available at the cash machine and our pizza delivered in 30 minutes or it's free. Most of us can find ourselves being impatient at times, not wanting to stand on lines and wait or expecting instant service were ever we go. Realistically, we live in a spoiled society receiving instant service may not always be possible. You see the pattern developing--you must make it as easy as you can for people to do business with you, regardless of the home business you operate.

14. Considerate of Client's Needs-

You must remain cognizant of the fact that few people will work hard, go out of their way, or be inconvenienced just for the privilege of giving you their hard-earned money. The shoe is always on the other foot. Making it easy for people to do business with you means that you must be accessible and knowledgeable about your products and services. You must be able to provide customers with what they want, when they want it. Customer service is not always an easy task, you may feel a customer is spoiled, a complainer or looking for a free deal. No matter if the case is true or not, sometimes it's not worth risking your sales or losing a loyal customer over small things, such as a coupon, free shipping or a free item that may have been promised as a deal. Remember to remain considerate.

15. Build A Firm Reputation.

A good reputation is unquestionably one of the home business owner's most tangible and marketable assets. People need to know that your service or product is reliable. They also need to know that you provide outstanding service to your customers or clients with their best interest at heart. You can't simply buy a good reputation; it's something that you earn by honoring your promises. If you promise to have the merchandise in the customer's hands by Wednesday, you have no excuse not to have it there. If you offer to repair something, you need to make good on your offer. Consistency in what you offer is the other key factor. If you cannot come through with the same level of service (and products) for clients on a regular basis, they have no reason to trust you . . . and without trust, you won't have a good reputation.

16. Sell yourself & Sell benefits.

Entrepreneurship is the only business where it's ok to sell yourself! When it comes to making money beyond the traditional 9-5 job many people are mastering and learning the art of becoming a product. Becoming a product means that you make yourself a brand to your consumers. People buy into you because they believe in your vision and your leadership. That's what sets the entrepreneur markets standards. That's why you can have hundreds of companies selling products and they are all making money. That should tell the neonate entrepreneur something, "there's enough money out there for all of us!"

Pushing product features is for inexperienced or wannabe entrepreneurs. Selling the benefits associated with owning and using the products and services you carry is what sales professionals worldwide focus on to create buying excitement and to sell, sell more, and sell more frequently to their customers. Your advertising, sales presentations, printed marketing materials, product packaging, website, newsletters, trade show exhibit and signage are vital. Every time and every medium used to communicate with your target audience must always be selling the benefits associated with owning your product or using your service.

17. *Get Involved.*

Always go out of your way to get involved in the community that supports your business. You can do this in many ways, such as pitching in to help local charities, nonprofits or the food bank, becoming involved in organizing community events, and getting involved in local politics. You can join associations and clubs that concentrate on programs and policies designed to improve the local community. It's a fact that people like to do business with people they know, like and respect, and with people who do things to help them as members of the community.

18. Grab Attention.

Small-business owners cannot waste time, money and energy on promotional activities aimed at building awareness solely through long-term, repeated exposure. If you do, chances are you will go broke long before this goal is accomplished. Instead, every promotional activity you engage in must put money back in your pocket so that you can continue to grab more attention and grow your business. Find new creative ways to spark the interest of you clients. Take advantage of any free marketing and resources opportunities such as social media, YouTube, get clients to post testimonials and reviews of your products or services to boost your exposure and reputation.

19. Master the art of Negotiations.

The ability to negotiate effectively is unquestionably a skill that every home business owner must make every effort to master. Negotiation comes in handy when making deals where your company has to spend money and it's also a skill that is profitable to have when customers know they can take their dollars elsewhere. Having the ability to negotiate can empower you to earn new clients, keep old clients and grow in profits. Negotiating perhaps second in importance only to asking for the sale in terms of home business musts. In business, negotiation skills are used daily. Always remember that mastering the art of negotiation means that your skills are so finely tuned that you can always orchestrate a win-win situation. These win-win arrangements mean that everyone involved feels they have won, which is really the basis for building long-term and profitable business relationships.

20. Design your workspace for success.

Carefully plan and design your home office workspace to ensure maximum personal performance and productivity and, if necessary, to project professionalism for visiting clients. If at all possible, resist the temptation to turn a corner of the living room or your bedroom into your office. Set up a space that gives you your own work space that's more appropriate and friendly for people to come and conduct business with you. Ideally, you'll want a separate room with a door that closes to keep business activities in and family members out, at least during prime business and revenue generating hours of the day. A den, spare bedroom, basement or converted garage are all ideal candidates for your new home office. If this is not possible, you'll have to find a means of converting a room with a partition or simply find hours to do the bulk of your work when nobody else is home where you will not run into disturbances and distractions.

21. Get and stay organized.

The key to staying organized is not about which type of file you have or whether you keep a stack or two of papers on your desk, but it's about managing your business. It's about having systems in place to do things. Therefore, you want to establish a routine by which you can accomplish as much as possible in a given workday, whether that's three hours for a part-time business or seven or nine hours as a full-timer.

In fact, you should develop systems and routines for just about every single business activity. Small things such as creating a to-do list at the end of each business day, or for the week, will help keep you on top of important tasks to tackle. Creating a single calendar to work from, not multiple sets for individual tasks or jobs, will also ensure that jobs are completed on schedule and appointments kept. Incorporating family and personal activities into your work calendar is also critical so that you work and plan from a single calendar. Once you have all of your activities and objectives in order it will be easy to manage what your day to day task and responsibilities are. Making time for family, the wife, husband or kids is very important. You don't want to spend so much time building your business that you neglect the people you love and support what you do. Even making time to be social is important, meeting with friends, mentors and associates that are supportive of you or just for social entertainment.

22. Take time off.

The temptation to work around the clock is very real for some home business owners. There are many entrepreneurs that dive head into their business without considering some of the pointers I ended with in number 21 of the laws of entrepreneurship. After all, you don't have a manager telling you it's time to go home because they can't afford the overtime pay. Every person working from home must take time to establish a regular work schedule that includes time to stretch your legs and take lunch breaks, plus some days off and scheduled vacations.

Create the schedule as soon as you have made the commitment to start a home business. Of course, your schedule will have to be flexible. You should, therefore, not fill every possible hour in the day. Give yourself a backup hour or two. All work and no play makes you burn out very fast and cantankerous customer service is not what people want.

23. Limit the number of hats you wear.

It's difficult for most business

owners not to take a hands-on approach. They try to do as much as possible and tackle as many tasks as possible in their business. The ability to multitask, in fact, is a common trait shared by successful entrepreneurs. However, once in a while you have to stand back and look beyond today to determine what's in the best interest of your business and yourself over the long run. I can personally tell you from a wealth of business experience, you cannot do it all yourself. Not only that but you must learn how to relinquish responsibilities to other staff members as well as train others to handle tasks that can alleviate you and allow to accomplish more. Most highly successful entrepreneurs will tell you that from the time they started out, they knew what they were good at and what tasks to delegate to others.

24. As for references

When you provide your customers with excellent service you should not be afraid of asking for references or referrals. You should also ask for testimonials, written or by video. This will help in building credibility and attract loyal customers who will genuinely appreciate your service product. Asking your customers to refer other family members and friends to your business will help you to grow at a fast pace. Everyone in business knows that one of the most successful ways to quickly grow and market your business is through good services and word of mouth recommendations. Another helpful tip considering the type of service you provide asking for reference letters or testimonials of how your service has helped your client will help grow your business as well as help you to gain new clients.

25. *Follow-up constantly.*

Constant contact, follow-up, and follow-through with customers, prospects, and business alliances should be the mantra of every home business owner, new or established. Constant and consistent follow-up enables you to turn prospects into customers, increase the value of each sale and buying frequency from existing customers, and build stronger business relationships with suppliers and your core business team. Follow-up is especially important with your existing customer base, as the real work begins after the sale. It's easy to sell one product or service, but it takes work to retain customers and keep them coming back.

Final Words

This book was never intended to be long. This book while it is short was written to pin point quick tips to help empower entrepreneurs and neonate entrepreneurs with wisdom and a resource that could be used as a guide for getting into the game of business.

With this mini book you have the basic information and tools needed to empower you to start a thriving business. Take them and implement them in your life. If you would like to read more in-depth about business I would suggest purchasing some of my other books on entrepreneurship like, "Called To Affluence", "The Newborn Entrepreneur", "Wealthy Minds", "Think Like A Millionaire" Or "The Millionaire Class" series.

Each of the above named books are powerful tools intended to reach different audiences. Its wisdom and insight that I have been privileged to put together from being mentored by millionaires as well as mentoring others in leadership and business.

Take the time to get acquainted with resources that will empower you to be a better and more skillful entrepreneur. Once you're more serious about building your business and your strengths things will begin to come naturally to you. Some say experience is the best teacher and indeed from experience you will grow. There's nothing like getting your feet and hands wet learning to grow and do what you do in a greater way.

Take a moment to share "The Laws of Entrepreneurship" with someone you know!

Other Books By The Author

1. Soul Cleanse Vol. 1 (Poetry)
2. Lost & Found (Poetry)
3. Life Editing Vol. 1- Taking Out The Trash
4. Called To Affluence
5. Diary Of An Ex Husband
6. Wealth & Abundance (Meditations for Prosperous Living)
7. The Millionaire Class Vol. 1
8. Prayerology Vol. 1- The School Of Prayer
9. The Purpose Driven Prayer Life

The Laws Of Entrepreneurship
Michael McCain

About The Author

Dr. Michael McCain, best known as a motivational speaker, author. Yet there's more to his experience and story Dr. McCain is also a poet, entrepreneur, life coach and spiritual teacher. Michael is also an established author of several books over the last 10 years and has grown in his experience to go from print press publishing to owning his own publishing company. Michael has a wide range of experience both in business and in the non-profit religious sector. Best known as the General in the Art of Strategic Prayer and Spiritual Warfare, The Author of "Prayerology" Michael McCain is a life coach, Prophetic voice and Ambassador of Hope.

Dr. Michael McCain is a 21st Century World Leader who has partnered with business moguls, politicians, church, civic and world leaders for more than 15 years to equip and empower millions to maximize their potential. As one of the leading voices of our time, he founded Dr. Michael McCain Enterprises Inc. (DMME), Maximize Publishing Inc. & Kaleo University, as well as a conglomerate of companies and business to bring practical solutions to spiritual and social ills; effecting change within our communities while transforming the course of our global destiny. His track record as a revolutionary thinker and prolific communicator, has established him as one of the most respected and sought-after youthful leaders in the world today.

Since 2010 Michael McCain has been a highly sought-after spiritual coach mentoring leaders, clergy and lay members. With his move in the publishing industry he has set himself apart not just to the church but to the world; making his life coaching experience broad enough to reach people in the pews as well as the secular marketplace. He has successfully made his mark with his books in Self Help and Empowerment as well as Spirituality and Entrepreneurship. His wisdom as insight is beyond his years and is a voice that will be remembered through generations.

www.ingramcontent.com/pod-product-compliance
Lightning Source LLC
Chambersburg PA
CBHW071639170526
45166CB00003B/1361